THE COMANCHE

A TRUE BOOK®

by
Christin Ditchfield

Children's Press®
A Division of Scholastic Inc.

New York Toronto London Auckland Sydney
Mexico City New Delhi Hong Kong
Danbury, Connecticut

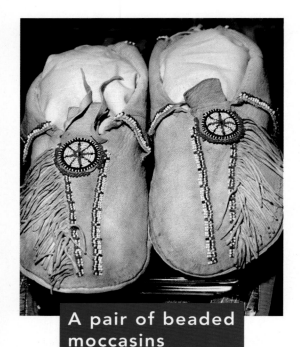

A pair of beaded
moccasins

Content Consultant
Liz Sonneborn

*The photograph on the title
page shows a Comanche man
wearing a traditional costume
at the Red Earth Festival in
Oklahoma City.*

Library of Congress Cataloging-in-Publication Data
Ditchfield, Christin.
    The Comanche / by Christin Ditchfield.
        p. cm. — (A true book)
    Includes bibliographical references and index.
    0-516-23644-X (lib. bdg.)   0-516-25590-8 (pbk.)
        1. Comanche Indians—Juvenile literature. I. Title. II. Series.
E99.C85D57 2005
978.004'974572—dc22   2004030922

CHILDREN'S PRESS, and A TRUE BOOK™, and associated logos are
trademarks and/or registered trademarks of Scholastic Library Publishing.
SCHOLASTIC and associated logos are trademarks and/or registered
trademarks of Scholastic Inc.

1 2 3 4 5 6 7 8 9 10 R 14 13 12 11 10 09 08 07 06 05

Contents

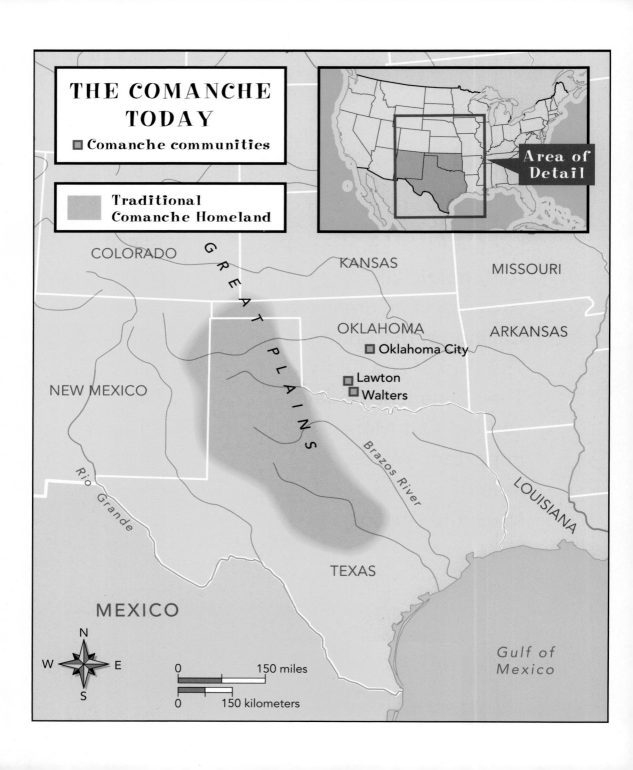

THE COMANCHE
TODAY
□ Comanche communities

Traditional
Comanche Homeland

Area of
Detail

COLORADO   KANSAS   MISSOURI

GREAT PLAINS

OKLAHOMA   ARKANSAS

□ Oklahoma City

NEW MEXICO   □ Lawton
                  □ Walters

Rio Grande   Brazos River

LOUISIANA

TEXAS

MEXICO

Gulf of
Mexico

N
W   E
S

0   150 miles

0   150 kilometers

Lords of the Southern Plains

For centuries, a tribe known as the Shoshone Indians traveled through the many valleys between the Sierra Nevada and the Rocky Mountains. This area is known as the Great Basin. The Shoshone did not settle in a particular part of this region.

Instead, they moved from place to place searching for food. Very little rain came over the high mountains, and the valleys were often as dry as deserts. Nothing grew in large amounts—or for very long. The land could not support many groups of people living in one place. There was simply not enough food or water.

Historians say that in the 1500s or 1600s, a group of Shoshone separated from the

The Comanche National Grassland in Colorado was home to the Comanche in the 1700s.

Artist Frederick Remington painted this portrait of a Comanche man on horseback.

tribe, moving south and east. They became known as the Comanche. Like the Shoshone, the Comanche traveled from place to place in search of food, good hunting, and warm weather. The Comanche protected their lands and added to their wealth by constantly going to war against other Indian tribes and European **settlers**. Over time, they gained control of a vast territory that included parts of Texas,

New Mexico, Oklahoma, Kansas, Colorado, and Mexico. They grew to be a proud and powerful people—the Lords of the Southern Plains.

The Comanche called them-selves *Nerm*, a word that means "people." It was the Ute Indians who nicknamed them *Koh-Mahts*, meaning "anyone who wants to fight me all the time." Spanish explorers spelled it *Komantcia*. In English, the word became *Comanche*.

A Comanche war party rides out to do battle.

A Nomadic Life

For more than two hundred years, the Comanche lived a **nomadic** life, moving from place to place. They became highly skilled horsemen and expert buffalo hunters. They followed the herds across the Great Plains, using spears or bows and arrows to capture their **prey**.

The Comanche were known for their excellent horsemanship.

The Comanche were famous for their amazing ability to lean over their horses' necks and fire their arrows from under the animals' chins. They did this while galloping at full speed!

The women of a Comanche village prepare buffalo skins for use as robes and dry buffalo meat for future meals.

The Comanche camped in cone-shaped tents called tepees. Tepees were made of buffalo skins stretched over long wooden poles. When the tribe needed to move on in search of food, these tents could be taken down quickly and later put back up just as quickly. The walls of the tepee were often decorated with painted patterns of shapes and symbols. Inside the tent, there was a platform for sleeping. Fires were used to keep the tents warm at night.

Comanche women made their families' clothing from

animal skins, usually deer or buffalo. Men wore leggings that were covered with breechcloths, which are aprons with front and back flaps that hang from the waist. Their battle clothes were colorful and detailed. Warriors wore headdresses and carried shields that were made of buffalo horns, feathers, bear teeth, and horsehairs.

Comanche women wore long deerskin dresses, which were decorated with paint, beads,

A group of Comanche men and women wear traditional dance clothing in this picture from the early 1900s.

and fringe. Both men and women wore leather shoes called moccasins. In the winter, they bundled up in buffalo-skin robes.

Growing Up Comanche

For the Comanche, life could be a daily struggle. Sometimes there wasn't enough food. Comanche warriors hunted for buffalo, elk, bear, antelope, and deer. They traded with other tribes for vegetables, such as corn and beans. They went to war to capture horses, guns, and food supplies.

A nutting stone was used to break open nutshells.

Comanche women gathered fruits, nuts, and berries. They used roots and herbs to make special stews. They took care of their family's everyday needs. Everyone worked together to help the tribe survive and prosper.

Comanche children were treated as precious gifts to the tribe. Sometimes during a raid, the Comanche captured children from other tribes or settlements. They lovingly raised these children as their own.

Because their parents were often busy working, Comanche children spent a lot of time with

A Comanche boy in a cradleboard, a carrier that can be used as a portable cradle or to carry a baby on one's back.

their grandparents. By imitating adult members of the tribe, children learned skills such as cooking, sewing, and making

Comanche children learned how to do many chores by watching and imitating their elders.

bows and arrows. They helped gather food and firewood. Most Comanche children could ride horses by the time they were four years old. They learned to take care of the horses, too.

The Hand Game

The Comanche had little time for singing, dancing, or playing games. But when they could relax and enjoy themselves, they often played one favorite game—the hand game.

In this game, several people secretly pass an object back and forth. Another person tries to guess who is holding the object. The game could go on and on for hours. It is still popular among the Comanche today.

Calling on The Spirits

The Comanche did not **worship** any one god or spirit, but they did believe in the spirit world. They believed spirit beings lived in rocks and animals, and they expressed their love and devotion to these spirits. The Comanche believed that if they pleased the spirits, the spirits

This shield, like many American Indian objects, is decorated with pictures of animals. These animals often represented spirit beings that deserved honor and respect.

would reward, protect, or provide for them.

The Comanche looked for spiritual guidance through visions and dreams. At one time or another, every young

A man drums during a peyote religious ceremony.

man would go out alone on a vision quest to discover what the spirits might say to him. He would then create his own medicine bundle, a container filled with

sacred objects that reminded him of his vision and of the powers the spirits had given to him.

In the 1800s, the Comanche began to practice the peyote religion. Followers gather together to sing, pray, and to take peyote, a drug made from the tops of cactus plants. This drug causes visions or **hallucinations**. Later, the Comanche formed the Native American Church to protect their right to practice this religion. Many Comanche belong to this church today.

The End of the Old Way

The Comanche came into contact with Spanish explorers as early as the 1600s. The explorers were soon followed by trappers, traders, settlers, and **missionaries**. By the 1800s, thousands of white settlers began moving across the Great Plains. Some of these

A covered wagon travels the Oregon Trail, a route taken by many white people as they made their way west.

settlers built their homes right in the middle of Comanche territory. Others passed through Comanche lands on their way to Oregon and California.

The land could not support all these people. In addition, wagon trains disturbed the **migrating** patterns of the buffalo. The natural environment as the Comanche had known it was destroyed. Food became even harder to find.

Unlike some neighboring tribes, the Comanche did not retreat or try to keep peace with the settlers. Instead, they fought fiercely to protect their lands and their way of life. They

A wagon train is attacked by a group of Comanche.

attacked forts and settlements.
They ambushed wagon trains.
For years, the Comanche waged

Chief Quanah Parker led many Comanche raids on white settlers.

war against the unwanted newcomers. They killed some and took others captive. The

U.S. Army and law enforcement officers known as the Texas Rangers came to defend the settlers. The Comanche defeated these forces time and time again.

Lack of food and disease, however, proved to be more powerful enemies. The Comanche once had as many as 20,000 people in the tribe. But sickness, starvation, and constant war took a terrible toll. By 1875, there were fewer than 1,500 Comanche left. They no longer had the strength to fight, so they surrendered to

Kiowa chief Lone Wolf set up camp at Fort Sill, Oklahoma, in 1875 after surrendering to the U.S. Army. The Kiowa had joined forces with the Comanche and other southern Plains Indian tribes. They could not defeat the soldiers and were forced to move onto reservations.

the U.S. Army and gave up their lands. The Comanche were forced to move onto **reservations** in Oklahoma.

Code Talkers

During World War II, a group of young Comanche men served in the U.S. Army as code talkers. They were sent to the battlefront in Europe, where they used a code based on their native language to communicate top secret information to different companies and commanders. They translated important messages into Comanche, to confuse the enemy and keep valuable information safe.

The Comanche language was so different from European languages that the German forces could not figure it out.

The Comanche Today

Today, there are about 12,000 Comanche in the United States. Some still live on the reservation they share with the Kiowa and Apache near Oklahoma City. Many have moved to cities in Oklahoma and Texas.

The Comanche live just like other Americans in many ways.

Wallace Coffey, a chief of the Comanche, dressed in shirt and tie.

They wear the same kinds of clothes and drive the same kinds of cars. They live in houses and apartment buildings. Some

Like many other American kids, these Comanche boys enjoy a game of basketball.

members of the tribe work as doctors, teachers, or lawyers. Some make a living by farming or breeding cattle. Others own businesses such as restaurants and hotels. Many young

Comanche men and women have chosen careers in the military. Though they live modern lives, the Comanche also work hard to preserve their history and **culture**.

Veteran's Day is a time to honor Comanche military men and women.

They want the next **generation** to understand all the joys and struggles of the past. They want their young people to know what it means to be Comanche.

An official Comanche language dictionary helps them preserve their language. There are newspapers and magazines that celebrate the Comanche way of life. Members of the tribe connect with one another and share their history through Web sites and online groups.

A group of Comanche in New Mexico celebrate their heritage.

A Comanche dancer in traditional clothing is ready to perform.

Every July, thousands of people from all over the country gather at the Comanche Homecoming Powwow in Walters, Oklahoma. Tribe members dress in traditional costumes. They perform ceremonial songs and dances and share traditional arts and crafts and recipes. There are rodeos, parades, and pageants. All of these activities help the Comanche people celebrate their past, present, and future.

To Find Out More

Here are some additional resources to help you learn more about the Comanche:

 **Books**

Birchfield, D. L. **Comanche.** Gareth Stevens, 2003.

DePaola, Tomie. **Legend of the Bluebonnet: An Old Tale of Texas**. Putnam Juvenile, 1996.

George, Charles. **The Comanche.** Gale Group, 2003.

Lund, Bill. **The Comanche Indians.** Capstone Press, 1997.

Shefelman, Janice Jordan, and Tom Shefelman. **Comanche Song.** Eakin Press, 2000.

Yacowitz, Caryn, and Carolyn Yacowitz. **Comanche Indians.** Heinemann Library, 2002.

Organizations and Online Sites

Colorado History—From Cliff Dwellings to Statehood
http://www.state.co.us/kids/ clchistory.htm

Log on to learn more about the history of the Comanche and other American Indian tribes in Colorado.

The Comanche Language and Cultural Preservation Committee
www.comanchelanguage.org

Visit this site to learn more about the Comanche language and the code talkers of World War II.

How the Buffalo Were Released on Earth
http://www.indians.org/ welker/buffalor.htm

Read a Comanche story that tells how the buffalo became scattered over Earth.

National Museum of the American Indian
Fourth Street and Independence Avenue SW Washington, DC 20024
202-633-1000
http://www.nmai.si.edu/

Visit the museum to learn more about American Indian history and culture.

The Texas Comanches
http://www.texasindians. com/comanche.htm

Log on to this site to learn more about the history of the Comanche in Texas.

Important Words

culture a way of life for a group of people

generation people born around a certain time

hallucination something you see in your mind that isn't real

migrating moving from region to region

missionaries people who travel to share their faith with others

nomadic moving from place to place

prey animals that are hunted for food

reservation land set aside by the government as a place for American Indians to live

sacred holy; having to do with religion; something deserving of great respect

settler a person who makes a home in a new place

worship to show love and devotion

Index

Meet the Author

Christin Ditchfield is an author, conference speaker, and host of the nationally syndicated radio program *Take It to Heart!* Her articles have been featured in magazines all over the world. A former elementary school teacher, Christin has written more than thirty books for children on a wide range of topics, including sports, science, and history. She makes her home in Sarasota, Florida.